BOOK MARKETING AND KEYWORDS

How to Sell More Books by Optimizing your Amazon Rankings

by

WALT POPESTER

Copyright © 2016 Walt Popester

All rights reserved. All rights reserved. No part of this publication may be reproduced, stored in a retrieval system, or transmitted in any form or by any means, electronic, mechanical, photocopying, recording, or otherwise, without prior permission of the author.

PUBLISHED BY:

WALT POPESTER
waltpopester@gmail.com

TO ALL THE DREAMERS OUT THERE

CONTENTS

	INTRODUCTION	09
1	FACTORS INFLUENCING RANKING	13
2	BOOK DESCRIPTION	35
3	PERMAFREE	45
4	REVIEWS	54
5	DRAW TRAFFIC	61
6	THE FLAG SHIP THEORY	69
7	COVER IMAGE	72
8	MAILING LIST	82
9	SELLING BOOKS INTERNATIONALLY	93

Introduction

(okay, you may skip it, but I do think it's better you read it)

Who am I? I'm Walt Popester and I wrote Dagger, a dark fantasy saga which is selling. Why am I telling you this? Because I think that there are too many people out there writing books about *selling books* and they don't sell nada. The first proof that you know what you're talking about, as a marketing expert, is to sell *your* books before you tell others how to sell theirs. I'm Italian and I decided to write this guide in English. So if you see some mistakes and typos be kind to me. Anyway, I suppose you're here for the information I can give you, not to test my English skills, and believe me: you're going to like this ride.

Why am I writing this? I used to sell zero, until I decided to learn the best strategies to sell my books. I soon became sick about people writing marketing books that don't tell anything really important, just some cheap info you may find everywhere on kdp guidelines. And they sell a lot, damn it. I studied a lot, made my homework, attended webinars and talked to people. In the end, I realized that if you can sell a dark fantasy saga in a universe so full of fantasy sagas, you do have a good knowledge about the market and it's time to help others to get where I am.

Why am I giving away my knowledge? I'm not giving it away. I'm selling it. All those books telling you absolutely nothing may be free, or 0.99. I'm selling at 2.99 which is a lot in this 0.99 world, and I consider it a fair price for my time and my suggestions. This book is short. You may find longer ones if you want. I just don't like to water down the information I can give you with useless chatter like a lot of kdp counselors do. Besides, Amazon sky is big enough for both you and me to be best-selling authors.

I'm going to give you the tips I used for my books and I promise I won't withhold any info in my possession, telling you something like: *you'll find the next tip in my next book*. No. I'm going to write only this marketing book, and do you know why? Because if I'm here, and if you are here, it's because we love books... and I can't wait to get back to write my fantasy series (and even because my readers are waiting and would kill me if I linger here too much).

So. The first thing you have to learn is what Amazon is. I'm not kidding. Think about it for a couple of seconds. Some of you are already thinking: the biggest bookstore on earth!

Red light: WROOOOONG!

If you want to make it work for you, begin to respect Amazon for what it is: a search engine. The second biggest search engine on earth, after Google. BUT. If I go on Google and type *American civil war* probably I don't mean to buy it. When you go on Amazon and type something, even *American civil war*, you're looking for something to buy. Always. Be it a book about Gettysburg or the action figure of President Abraham Lincoln, you're on Amazon because you mean to spend some bucks on something. And this makes a lot of difference, as you can easily understand.

Believe me, this means *gold rush*.

But what will decide your ranking on the search results among the millions of books out there, and how can you climb to the top?

Uh uh uh (satanic laughter). Sit down my friends and have a drink.

We begin.

Factors influencing rankings

You may already know some of the things I'm talking about here, I know. If you're here, after all, you are a pro or someone who is struggling to get to the top and I appreciate that. You're great. But I think I will surprise you.

What are the most important factors that will influence your ranking in the search results? Easy: reviews, the right keywords, the right PLACE for keywords (this is the most interesting part. You will see), your ranking in your subgenre, your price. Amazon will never tell you which one is more important than the others, but since we can work on all of them, it's really pointless to wonder.

We're going to cover all of them, of course, but I'm going to focus on the most important one:

Keywords.

We all know that kdp allows us to use up to seven keywords for each of our books. We all know that they don't have to be single words, and that it's proved that short sentences work better than single words (for instance, *dark fantasy kindle books* will probably work better than *fantasy*, simply because fantasy is overused). Keywords are the words used by costumers to *look for things to buy on Amazon*. Simple. Choosing the right keywords will bring you to intercept costumers right where they are looking for you.

Of course, the keywords working better are the ones having a high relevance to your book. I won't use *marketing strategies* for my fantasy books only because *marketing strategies* has a lot of traffic, right?

Good.

There are a lot of software that may help you in choosing the keywords that will work better for you, be your book fiction or non fiction. Many agree that **Kindle Samurai** is one of the best. I can't know for sure, I don't get paid from them, so I'm not going to tell you this software is the best, but I will tell you that it's the one that I use and that I'll never change, and never regret having used.

You may find all the info about the product here: http://kindlesamurai.net/ I'm not going to waste your time telling you things explained much better in the short and practical demonstrative video on their site. Spend a couple of minutes on it, it's very useful, then come back here.

Remember that you can do all this *manually* on Amazon, typing a keyword in the Amazon search bar and then scrolling through the search results. You may have realized, though, that if you have to do it for thirty, or one hundred, keywords it will take you *centuries*.

Kindle Samurai will save you a lot of time, and time means money, since we have other books to write, edit, publish (and sell) but only one, short mortal life to do everything. It will look for the keyword you typed and its *related search terms*, or *suggestions*, that is to say other keywords that are related to the one you chose.

For instance, if you type *fantasy*, and click *search* on the *kindle search engine suggestions* you'll get this:

fantasy romance

free fantasy books

fantasy erotica

free fantasy kindle books

urban fantasy

science fiction and fantasy

fantasy free

fantasy series

These are all related keywords that you can use as one of the seven keywords of your book. Kindle Samurai will show you dozens of them, hundreds of them, analyze them and tell you in which one you will have less competition.

Why do you want less competition? To show higher, of course. You don't want to end up in a search result together with other forty thousands books. You'd prefer the company of 1000 book, or less. Well, Kindle Samurai will tell you how.

One thing that this guys are not telling you, anyway, is that Kindle Samurai is pretty useless if you don't know how many users are looking for those precise keywords every month. Okay, you have only 1000 competitors for *fantasy with a lot of sex in it*, but if only two hundred people per month are typing that on the Amazon search bar it's pretty useless, you follow me?

Their developers suggest to combine Kindle Samurai with Google Adwords, a free service of Google that tells you how many Google users are looking for that keyword every month.

Tsk. I've got a better solution. So we get to…

TIP number 1!

There's a web software that tells you how many users, every month, are searching for a keyword on **Amazon**. Is it better? Of course it is better than Google Adwords, because it refers to Amazon itself! (remember what I wrote about American civil war, right?) The software\website I'm talking about is called https://www.merchantwords.com/ go and check it out. It's not free, you have to pay a little bit every month to use it. BUT. You get five *free* attempts everyday (of course–and I'm not *telling* you to do this–if you could change your IP you may get more than five everyday…).

Again, I don't get royalties from them. These are just the two software I use to sort out keywords.

Sounds complicated? It's not. I'm taking *fantasy* for example throughout this book. Fantasy is a big pond; way too big. It will show you almost 160.000 books and believe me: no one can afford such competition. It's wrong to use *fantasy* as a single keyword if you're not Martin. Now, we want to narrow *fantasy* down to something more specific, a little pond where our little book will show higher. This is why related keywords are important.

As you can see on merchantwords.com, you can adjust the search results in some way. After the first research–that you can't change–you will see three windows: *search term* on the left, *category* in the middle and *sort by* on the right. I suggest you select *kindle* as *search category*, since we want to know how that keyword is doing in the *kindle store*, not *digital music, electronics* or such. Then I suggest you sort the results by highest search volume (because we want to know which of the related keywords are the most popular).

Write fantasy again. So we get:

fantasy baseball,

fantasy basketball,

fantasy books for adults,

fantasy books for teens,

fantasy books for kids age 9 12.

Wow. I don't know what to do with the first ones, but look at the third, fourth, and fifth search results, each one with a 655,000 estimated monthly search volume. It's a lot of people, and you have narrowed down your search to something more specific. Of course you have to find something that will do with the content of your book. For instance, I may choose *fantasy books for adults*, for Dagger, but not for *kids age 9 12*. It's a dark fantasy, I don't want to be sued by angry mothers.

If I search for these terms with Kindle Samurai, the software will tell me in which one I have a greater possibility to show higher.

Find keywords related to your field and see how they go on merchantwords. Then put them on Kindle Samurai to see with which ones your book may show higher (or you may do the contrary).

Have fun. It doesn't take long once you find your way, and it will be a good use of your time.

When you find a keyword with a high search volume (merchantwords) and with little competition (Kindle Samurai) you can shout: BINGO! Pick it, write it in your *keywords* window during the publishing process of your book on kdp, and your sales\downloads will increase in a matter of hours after having saved and published.

Again. **It's better to be a big fish in a little pond than the other way around: a little fish in a big pond.** Even because once you see that your pond has become too little, you may jump and get to a slightly bigger one, and so on, as your audience grows month by month.

Play with both software, learn how to use them, it will take time. One thing that I've learned is that the best ideas come to mind after having spent some time on them.

Now. That was just the beginning. We said that you can choose up to 7 keywords. Believe me: I lied. This is not true.

This is one of the great tips I'm going to give you with this book, so open up your ears. Are you ready?

No. Really. I want to hear you say it. ARE YOU READY?

TIP number 2!

What no one will ever tell you, if you don't find it out by yourself, is that you can choose up to seventh keywords, right... but you can use up to 350 characters, divided by 7.

How much is that? I will show you. It's like this:

ccccc cc,cccccccc cc ccc,cccc cccc,ccc ccc,ccccccc

cc ccc,ccc ccc,cc ccccc ccc cccc ccc cc ccccc cccc

ccccc ccccccc cccc ccccccccccc ccccc ccccccc cccccc

ccccccc cccc ccccccccc ccccccc ccccc cccccc cccccc

cccc ccccc cccccc ccc ccccccccc cccc cccc ccc cccc

cccccc ccccc ccccccc ccccccc cccccc cccc cccc cccc

ccc cccc cccc cccccc cccccc ccccc ccccccc cccc ccc

I'm not going mad. I just wanted you to get a *visual proof* of what it means. It's HUGE. You see? The keywords may be long like that, and contain a LOT of single-word keywords. It's not forbidden from Amazon at the time this book is written. This means that you can use seven LONG keywords containing all the one-word keywords that you want. Count them, how many are they? Something between forty and fifty. Well, each one of those extra words can get you into an extra search results with thousands of people seeing your book.

And they can be combined too. If you wrote a book about cooking you may choose *pizza pasta spaghetti cooking recipes* as a part of your seventh keyword. You will show up not only in *pizza*, or *pasta*, search results, but even in *pasta recipes*. Amazon will mix them up for you. This thing alone is worth the money you spent with this book; if correctly used, it will get you far.

Really far. Practically, everywhere you want.

What if I told you that it doesn't stop here, that you can use even more than 350 characters for your keywords; that you could use 700 characters, or 1050, or even more?

I'm not mad. You can do it if you have a saga, or a series of books linked to each other. Again, this works best if you use that wonderful option that Amazon gives us: having a permafree book. Use your best keywords on book one (possibly a permafree one) than use **different** keywords for book two and three and so on. These books will show up into different search results, drawing more traffic to your production, to your series. In easy words: consider your saga of three books as one book with 1050 characters-worth of keywords.

Of course, this could be pretty useless to your potential readers if they haven't read book 1… so here's a tip. At the very beginning of your other books' descriptions write something like this, capital letters: **DOWNLOAD BOOK 1 FOR FREE!** (or discounted ad 0.99, something catchy. We'll talk how to use italics or bold characters in a minute.)

Many of them will actually look for book 1 and download it. You're right, my friends: more traffic to your books, and more money.

There are some words that people often write in the Amazon search bar, like *books ebooks series saga diaries novels kindle chronicles* and so on. I suggest you put the most fit of them in the famous seven keywords. Amazon search engine will use them combined with the other, more specific, keywords you chose and that will lead to you showing up in search results you probably didn't even imagined. *Pizza book*, for instance, if someone is looking for it.

Cool stuff, isn't it?

Always keep your eyes open. Experiment, be curious about stuff, never get sick of learning something new every day.

BEWARE!

Amazon has a very strict policy about choosing keywords and it's all here:

https://kdp.amazon.com/help?topicId=A2EZES9JAJ6H02

You CANNOT use keywords that are not related to your books. For instance, don't even try to type *twilight*. You'll get a mail by kdp telling you to be careful as soon as you click on save and publish. They say not to use words as *book* or *ebooks*, but I think theirs is more a suggestion than anything else, since a lot of people are actually using it without getting into trouble.

You wrote a fantasy with, let's say, time travel, fast horses and a lot of heavy violence? You can write: *time travel horses heavy violence* as a part of your seventh keywords. Just like that. More search results. More traffic. More money.

Just don't write *twilight*, please.

Now. I don't know for sure, but it may be that placing a keyword as the first or the sixth of your lot may be like telling Amazon that it is more important regarding the book, so your book may show even higher there.

A lot of people are using this TIP of the 350 keywords, but not everybody is telling you. It's like a secret, but it's no secret at all because you just need to type as long as you can in the keywords window to realize what happens. I want to share this knowledge because I like to keep a promise, when I tell you that your money was well spent with me.

Do you think your job is done?

Red light: WROOOOONG!

What I learned is that choosing the right keywords is just part of the game, maybe the most important, maybe not, but there are other factors that will get you up on the Amazon search results.

Remember when I talked about **placing** your keywords in the right places? Just get back to Kindle Samurai for a while. You'll see they consider some factors to tell you if your book has any chance to show in the first search results of a given keyword. One of them is marked as *KT* and one as *KD*.

KT will tell you how many books in the first page of that search result have that keyword in their *TITLE*. *KD* will tell you how many books have that keyword in their BOOK DESCRIPTION.

Why is Kindle Samurai so impatient to tell us this?

It's called *relevance* and it's way more important than what you may think. Having your keyword both inside your title *and* in your book description will turn into a better rank in the search result for that keyword.

What is *relevance*? It means how much your book is relevant to the keywords typed by the costumers in the Amazon search bar (to put it simple: Amazon understands that the keyword is *relevant* if that keyword is in the book title and in the book description, too).

There are a lot of ways to influence relevance, and to bring your book up, but I have to tell you again: be sure you don't go against kdp rules. These guys are very strict, and they are right to be so. You have to use keywords that are related to your books, I'll never get tired of saying this. Don't use *Game of thrones* if you're selling a fantasy book and you're not Martin; sooner or later they'll find out. They may be kind and comprehensive the first times, but they will eventually get tired of you and you don't want to be kicked out of Amazon. You don't want to be kicked out of the gold mine, right?

So be honest about it.

Now. Your book has a title, a subtitle, an author name, names of other people who worked on the book, a synopsis, editorial reviews, reviews, and... okay, I think that's it. This will bring us to our...

TIP number 4!

In the case one of your *keywords* show up in the title of your book, too, your book will show higher in the search results than those that don't have it. For instance. If one of your keywords is *fantasy book* (okay, it's just an example, right?) and if the title of your book is *Enchanted lands*, you could consider to name it: *Enchanted lands–a fantasy book*.

I assure you. *Enchanted lands–a fantasy book* will always show higher that *Enchanted lands*. This is why at times you see books called like that.

This is *gold*, guys. Give it the right importance. Be creative, trying not to break Amazon rules.

Sometimes we run across books like 'Gothika–a tale of vampires best horror book very good book oh my god how beautiful is my book'.

This is wrong. So terribly wrong. Not only it goes against the rules, but it looks bad and not professional. If I were a buyer and had to buy this, I'd skip. This may be a tip or not, but always, ALWAYS, give your product a decent overall look.

One of the most important rules that Amazon tells you not to break is that the title of your book must be shown on your cover image. So if you decide for *Enchanted lands–a fantasy book* please be sure the same thing is written on your cover image too.

Even your author name is a keyword, whether you like it or not. Amazon says you can use a pen name, and you can be a little creative even about this, but again: don't be stupid. Don't write *best fantasy* as co-author (it's not a joke, I swear some people do it!). It doesn't look professional and you want a product that is staying out there for decades, so don't spoil your name.

I know about some people who have chosen important names as surnames of their pen names. Ok, it sounds complicated, so here's an example. I may call myself: *John Paul King* or *Alfred Jack Martin*. I don't know if it is forbidden or not. What I know is of a writer who used this trick to climb the related search results and then got a lot of bad reviews saying how wrong it is to call yourself like that.

And bad reviews will bring you down. And bad reviews are the one thing you will never be able to change once they are there, so be careful: never break a kdp rule and always try to be professional.

Now. We have a book description, right? So ask me: has the book description anything to do with the search results of a keyword? Ask me.

Of course it has, this is why (as we were saying) Kindle Samurai tells you if in the top 12 of a keyword search results there are books with that keywords in their book descriptions.

If you have *fantasy book* (it's an example, it can be *fast cars* or *how to cook the best pizza*) in your book descriptions it will help get you higher. If you use it **several times** in your book description it will get you even higher. Again, you don't want your book description to look something like *A fantasy book that has a lot of fantasy, since it is a fantasy book* just to repeat the *fantasy* keyword. Be clever. Be creative.

I feel someone is asking for a tip here. A BIG tip. So, here we go.

TIP number 5!

At the end of your book description, you can add something like: **book categories:** *fantasy, epic fantasy, dark fantasy, superhero fantasy books* and so on. This way you will repeat your keywords all the times you want, and readers\buyers won't even notice, since it's more that probable that they won't even read that section of your book description, especially if you put it a little farther to the bottom (just using spacing).

Believe me. This will help you show higher.

There is a ratio between the total word count of your book description and the number of times a keyword is repeated. Let's say, a *concentration* of that keyword that is expressed in %, like: the 5% of your book description is made of the word *fantasy*. A ratio of 5% will show a higher relevance than a book description with a ratio of 3% for that keyword.

Of course it all has a cumulative power: if a keyword shows in your title, and in your book description too, with a high ratio, your book will have more relevance for that keyword itself compared to other books. Of course you have 350 characters and 7 keywords to use and you can't use them all together (did I already say look professional?), so it's up to you to decide which.

Try more than once. Try some combinations, wait some days to see how it works, and change again.

I'll probably end up writing this whole book about keywords, because they are the most powerful factor of all. Not the only one you have to work on, but surely the most powerful. We know that the times a keyword is repeated in your reviews has some importance, too, but not as much as the ones in your book description.

When you use Kindle Samurai and Merchant words, remember that results will vary over time, so let's say, once a week, or a month, use these software again to see if a keyword is still used or not, or if you have gained some opponents in your field and need to change.

I suggest you use the Amazon search bar every week for every one of your keywords (or combination of keywords) to see where you show up. If you see that your book shows on page 5 or 6 of a particular keyword, you may need to change it to something more useful, or to one with which you have less competition.

You can change keywords as much as you want, Amazon won't care until you respect their rules.

Do you think this is all?

Tsk.

We were saying.

Remember what I told you about being a little fish in a pig pond? If you type *fantasy* on Amazon search bar you will get 159,509 results at the time this book is written. If you're not Martin and I'm not Tolkien, we're the little fishes and yes, we're in big trouble.

But. I'm a pretty big fish in the *metaphysical and visionary fantasy*, or the *superhero fantasy*. These are called subgenres: the little ponds. Of course, I know I'm not talking to a fantasy writers audience, and you may have written a book about cooking pizzas, but it's the same. There's a big category that is *kindle ebooks*, at the top of which you will get once you sell TONS of books. Then there are other subgenres, ponds getting little and more little the more you get to the bottom of the ladder.

Even if most authors don't even know this (we know the 70% of them), Amazon doesn't make a secret of the way to get into these subgenres. Here: https://kdp.amazon.com/help?topicId=A200PDGPEIQX41
Amazon tells you which keyword to use to get into a specific subgenre. Once you know this, you're already ahead of 70% of kdp authors out there. Of course, be polite, clever and honest again: DON'T get into a subgenre if you don't have anything to do with it, just to show up in more search results possible.

For instance, I wrote a dark fantasy, okay, there's a lot of epic in it, good, and it has a strong philosophical component; there are a lot of visions in it, there are swords and magic. So I can get into *dark fantasy*, *metaphysical and visionary*, *sword and sorcery*, and *epic fantasy*. Choosing *dark fantasy* will get me into *horror*, too, which is a good pond for me. Now, in my book I've got a lot of people being slaughtered, graphic violence and a satanic god, so it's okay to be in *horror*, too. I will NEVER get into *norse*, or *christian fantasy*, just because these subgenres have tons of readers. I don't have vikings in my books, I can't do it, it's wrong.

Do the same. Choose the right subgenres. If you don't, it will take some time to Amazon to catch you, because first someone has to buy your book in the wrong section, get angry, write to Amazon and say: *Hey, this is not Christian Fantasy, what is this book doing in this section? IT IS WRONG!* some Amazon worker will take a look at it and realize it's right. It will take time, of course. But as the

Blondie song goes, *One way, or another, I'm gonna find you, I'm gonna get ya get ya get ya.*

Rules are important, don't be a pirate.

Of course there are some subgenres, let's say *coming of age*, or *young adults*, for which you have to use one of the six first keywords, since they are precise combinations of words. But for some of the others you can use just one word and you can use the famous seventh, long keyword for it.

I know for sure that you can end up into 20 subgenres maximum. Know that they depend on the main category you choose when you publish or upload a new version of your book. Be careful to get in the right ones, and not in too many, because Amazon will then decide arbitrarily in which ones you will end up, and maybe you will end up in the poor ones, sacrificing better possibilities.

What I recommend is to use two different BIG genre (for instance, *Fantasy* and *Action and Adventure*, or *Thriller Suspense*) with different subgenres specific for the two main categories. It's widely considered a big mistake to choose, for instance, *Dark Fantasy* and *Epic Fantasy* together as MAIN genres. Because it's like choosing only one genre, and this means less possibilities (but it can be a choice, if you're focusing only on fantasy, or on a specific main genre. You can always try different solutions and see what works best for you; that is generally my favorite suggestion: if it works even if everybody tells you it shouldn't work, than just do it).

Is this all?

Of course not.

Let's get back to the book description for one of the best tips of this section.

Book Description

First: how do you write a book description?

Really, that's the wrong question. The real question is:

What's the goal of a book description? To sell more books. Easy. It doesn't have anything to do with the quality of your book, just like the cover image: you have to use that in a way to grab readers' attention and that's the end of it. Of course grammar is fundamental: if you show mistakes or typos in your blurb, then readers will expect the same inside the book too and this won't be a great incentive to *buy* the book.

This being said, let's see the anatomy of a book description, that's exactly what will bring you to sell more.

As an ebooks writer I started with Smashwords, before Amazon realized the great potential of the ebooks market. On Smashwords you had (well, you still have) two separate fields for your book description: the short book description (or short pitch) and the long one. That's genial.

Do the same on Amazon: a short, punchy, above-the-fold tagline in which you write something very catchy (of course, it would be great if this could be in **bold** characters. We'll get to that in a short time). Then a little space. Then the long book description.

Authors often don't use taglines, which is a mistake in the mobile age, where only a few lines of description text are displayed. Your blurb must be catchy since the first line, just like a book must be catchy since the first paragraph.

Too many writers think of the blurb as a summary of what happens in the book. Come on, someone even tell us how the book is going to end!

That's wrong, of course. We don't care about the story when we're reading a blurb (think about your own experience). We want to know if we will suffer with the protagonist. We want to be told that we won't be able to put that book down until it's finished. We want promises and we want those promises to be kept. So use feelings. Use strong emotions: anger, passion, wrath. Use something that doesn't leave readers indifferent.

We want to find, then, what I call the *exotic* element: that one element that your book alone has. So let's say you have the blurb of a fantasy book that begins to talk about dragons, quests, knights, magic swords, magic rings, magic shoes, magic yaaaaaawn. Come on, there are a millions of book like that nowadays. What's the exotic element? What's that thing that makes your fantasy stand out and breaks with tradition?

It depends on your book, of course, but try to find one (or even better: try to think about it when you *write* the book). For Dagger 1, I wrote something like this: *I wrote a dark fantasy whose purpose was to break with tradition, the narrative addressing more existential issues rather than the old and overused formula of evil against good. In Dagger, the struggle between good and evil is not clear, nor easily identifiable. It is a tormented process, internal to the protagonist, with an outcome that is difficult to predict. I do not sell pre-cooked messages to the reader. I decided to create a story with multiple interpretations.*

I'm making a promise. I'm telling you: *Hey, this is something different, want to give it a try? It's free, come on, grab your copy. No evil vs good stuff anymore.*

Equals more traffic. As you can see in my blurb I wrote this in what is called a *Selling Paragraph*. After your blurb, spend a few lines to talk directly to your potential readers.

Few authors use this. It's also an opportunity to let folks know if the book is part of a series.

Do you want to be even more direct?

Call them to action. Most authors end their description with a synopsis and hope the reader will scroll up and buy. Nay. Use a CTA (Call To Action). *Ask* the reader to buy the book; this improves the chances of it happening.

Examples of a strong CTA is: *Buy this book and forget everything about the other fantasy books you read until today.*

Be creative. Look for the right balance between sarcasm, prestige and firmness.

Now, let's get to the technical matters.

Have you ever seen the bold writings, the orange ones, the big ones and the BIGGER ones? This is why Amazon allows you to use HTML coding in your description.

If you want a determined section of your description to look **bold** you have to type it like this:

I want this bold

and it will look like this:

I want this bold

Great, right? Not only will this give you a better graphic presentation of your product, but also…we'll talk about it later.

There are other three codings you can use to make your writing look bigger, BIGGER, or even BBIIIGGGEEERR!!

It's like this:

<h3>big</h3>

<h2>bigger</h2>

<h1>BIGGER</h1>

You can do something similar even with your author central profile. (go here if you don't know what it is: https://authorcentral.amazon.com/) but I found out that whenever you upload a new version of your book, these changes are gone and you have to go back every time to author central to change it. This can be *really* boring if you upload a new version of your book or you just change some keywords very often, like I do. So I suggest you change your book description and use HTML coding on your book *directly* on your kdp profile. You can even use this SUPERMEGAFANTASTIC free tool I found here http://kindlepreneur.com/amazon-book-description-generator/ give it a try, it's just great.

Experiment with it and find the best result possible, aesthetically speaking. I suggest you use HTML coding to highlight keywords. Not only to catch the reader's attention, as we said, but even because Amazon and Google will notice, too.

Not everybody does this and that's a mistake. Your Amazon product page can be searched even with Google and, to put it simple, if you use BIG words for some keywords both Amazon and Google will think those keywords have a high relevance related to your product.

Do you know what will happen? Of course: you will show higher in the search results than all those who are not using this method, and you will sell more.

Drawing traffic from outside Amazon is important. For now, just try to experiment with the HTML tips I gave you.

Now. **How can Amazon understand if a keyword is right for your book** (and how can you use this to climb the ladder of that search result)**?**

People are using a lot of keywords that don't have anything to do with their books. They're making a wrong use of them.

The URL of your product page (you do know what a URL is, right?) changes depending on the keyword your costumer has used to get to your product. We can say, that the keyword is included in the URL.

If I reach *Dagger* after having typed *free fantasy kindle books* in the Amazon search bar, my URL will look like this: http://www.amazon.com/gp/product/B00KTR8C90?keywords=f

ree%20fantasy%20kindle%20books&qid=1453634546&ref_=sr_1_22&sr=8-22

Click on it, so you can see it better.

Did you click? Well, very good. This will tell Amazon that that keyword works for my book (thank you for your help!). Clicking on this hyperlink, the one with the keywords in it, as you can see, will tell Amazon that someone has typed those keywords in the Amazon search bar, scrolled through the results, seen my book and clicked on it. This will tell Amazon: *hey, high relevance here!*

This would be perfect if that reader would buy the book, or download it, and review it 5 stars. That would be even more *positive reinforcement*. It sounds complicated, I know. The thing is, if I send this same link inside a facebook chat to a reader and tell him to see it, It would be like if he typed the keywords in the Amazon search bar to get to my product.

What do we have to earn from this? Everything, my friends. Telling Amazon that our book has a high relevance related to that keyword, will make us rise to the heavens in the search results.

Of course, if it's not just a reader but TONS of readers you will get higher and higher, straight to the skies.

How can you use this in a legitimate way? When you send the link to your book to readers, reviewers, facebook pals use a link with one your favorite keywords (possibly, the one with the highest traffic).

This will make the difference, believe me.

So, are we done with places where to place our keywords?

WROOOONG.

There's one last place that no one considers, but that has some relevance to the Amazon algorithm, even though I don't think it's that important (Amazon will never tell us, for sure). You know when you upload a file as a cover image? That file has a name. Well, you can place keywords even there. No one will know but you and Amazon. Again, this will even help to draw traffic from outside, with Google search results.

Now I think you know why my product page looks something like this: http://www.amazon.com/Dagger-Light-World-Fantasy-Adventure-ebook/dp/B00KTR8C90/ref=cm_cr_pr_product_top?ie=UTF8

These tips work both with free books and with pay books.

The first episode of Dagger is permafree (we will cover how to make a book permafree and how to use this wonderful option

Amazon is giving us, don't worry). It used to *sell* no more than 10 or 15 free copies everyday. When I made these changes I could see the sales diagram in my kdp dashboard skyrocket on the first day, and then grow everyday as well as my Amazon rankings to a respectable 100\150 copies per day. Of course, we may call it a basal rhythm, the copies I download when I'm not using other marketing strategies we'll cover later (that is to say: the days when I'm on holiday and the book is working for me, buying me a ice cold beer on the beach).

This is exactly what you want: a system that will work for you once everything is settled. Not only because we want to stuff our bank account with money, but also because when we were kids we wanted to become writers, great writers, and to be a writer you must have readers, you can't escape from that, even if most authors tend to forget. This thing is not only about sky-rocketing your sales page and watch the green or red spikes. This is about having more readers to share our art, our passion, more readers writing to us telling that they loved the book. THIS is my real purpose and should be yours too. Of course, like Stephen King once wrote, if someone signs a check for you, you must turn it into money. But that's not our first purpose, and surely that was not our first step. As I know for sure that the first time you picked up a pen or wrote the first characters on a computer screen, money was the last thing you were thinking about. When we were kids, remember? When all this began.

We want to be read. To be read is to be loved.

Permafree

So, let's talk about this matter: **why permafree?**

A permafree book in the Amazon *slang* means a book that is permanently free. You know that Amazon doesn't allow this easily, that is to say you can't set the price of your book to zero on the second page of your publishing process, where you have to choose the price on all the Amazon stores.

But you can still do it, if you know how.

Of course I'm telling you how, but first: why I, as well as many others kdp marketing counselors, think it is so important to have a permafree book in your army?

Easy: the whole web, and Amazon users themselves, are hungry for free products. They will download almost everything that is free, surely more than they will ever read. I'm okay with that: it gives you a chance to reach them, so play well. It was easy for me: I have a dark fantasy pentalogy, that is to say a saga with five books. I set the first book permafree, so everyone can have a free taste of the saga before buying the rest of the series.

Many won't read the book at all.

Many will read it, but won't buy the second book.

Some will read it and tell me that I suck, writing a 1-2 star review and trying to destroy my life with their hatred because surely I didn't waste their money, but I wasted their precious time.

Many will buy the second book, telling me that I'm great. Many of my readers told me that they met Dagger ONLY because the first book was free, and liked it so much to buy the other books (someone even wrote it in his\her reviews, as you can easily see).

That meant that this system brought me a reader that I wouldn't get otherwise. So I didn't give him\her a book for free: I sold him the following four books and we were both happy with that.

Your permafree book must be so good that it attracts people, has them read you to the end, and lead them to buy whatever else you're selling. I'm a *strong* permafree fan, I built my success with it in Italy and I'm planning to do the same even on the other stores.

You can do it with fiction, like me, and with non fiction. I think, though, this works best with fiction and with sagas, but all the marketing counselors out there are using this method, too, writing a short essay about keywords, for instance, in the hope you buy the rest of their manuals. No one is so crazy to write a single book-marketing book.

Okay, no one but me, but I already gave you my reasons.

Before we talk about the rest, this brings us to something I didn't want to say before. I wanted to begin with this *sort of* tip, but I thought that it would have decreased your attention. Well, the first tip, the most important one, is to learn how to write and sell the best product possible.

Well, okay thanks Walt, we all knew that.

Of course you did. You know because, just like me, you see that Amazon is so full of poorly edited products, too short products, products with a horrible cover image and so on. There are books with mistakes in the product description itself (some with mistakes in the *title* itself!). This is unacceptable in my humble opinion, and sooner or later will lead Amazon to change their policy on indies. There's your name on your book: make it good. Have it edited and proofreaded by a professional; don't wander in the web looking for cheap images but have a book cover worthy of this name drawn by an artist.

I know what this means: you have to pay for it. Well, do it. People are giving away their work and there are very good services out there in the web for some hundreds bucks; you don't have to spend millions. If you can spend 2000 bucks for a good editing, good for you, but if you can't, you can always find something fit to your wallet (no shame in that, I did the same in the beginning. As my sales grew, I could afford better collaborators and paid them. Do the same).

We all want to get in the top 100, right? But there's no easy way to do it, no trick that will allow you to skyrocket from ground zero to heaven. Getting there is a life commitment, and at some point (like I'm understanding just know) you have to begin to spend real money, the green ones. Simple as that.

Look professional, because you see: I may even tell you how to maximize the use of keywords, I can tell you how to reach hundreds of readers everyday, but if you're selling a bad product no one can help you. No one. The book people will see and buy and read will be a cheap one, and sooner than not you'll end up with ten bad reviews that will make our book sink before you can even realize what's happening.

So, how to make a book permafree? This is my method. The book has to be on a store different from Amazon. I use http://smashwords.com, that distributes my book to Apple, Kobo, B&N and other minor stores. I don't sell anything on them because I don't care, Amazon is my world, but I need this to prove to Amazon that I'm selling this product elsewhere, where is free, because Smashwords do allow you to set your price to 0.00. So what do we do then? We go to our authorcentral profile (the one we already saw talking about HTML coding), to our author page.

We look for the book we want permanently free and click on *contact us*.

BEWARE!

Use the *contact us* in the light blue window, because it has all the information on that book, that Amazon needs. Do not use the one on white background at the very bottom of the page, because it doesn't refer to your book, but to your general author profile.

So, you tell them: *Hi there. My book 'Dagger-The Light at the End of the World' is free on apple store (or whatever) at this link* (please, be sure you give them the exact link where they can find the free book, or it's going to be a mess. They receive thousands of request everyday and they surely don't waste their time downloading Itunes to look for your book on Apple store). *Please set this book permafree on Amazon.com/Amazon.uk/Amazon.ca/Amazon.au too. Bye, thanks* or something like this.

Now, if you want your book to be free even on, let's say, Amazon.de (Amazon store in Germany), you have to provide them with a Germany link to your book, otherwise your book will be free only on Amazon.com. I suggest you make it free worldwide, because Amazon is growing everywhere and every market has its possibilities. I suggest you use the Apple store for this particular matter, because you can easily change the URL. Maybe you won't have problems with Germany, but I assure you Brazil, Mexico and Japan will be harder.

This is the link to my book on apple store in italy: https://itunes.apple.com/it/book/dagger-light-at-end-world/id967516696?mt=11

Do I want to change it to a, let's say, Brazil one?

Easy. I just need to change the */it/* with the */br/* (or *fr* for France, *jp* for Japan and so on). So it will look like this:

https://itunes.apple.com/br/book/dagger-light-at-end-world/id967516696?mt=11

Or let's talk japanese:

https://itunes.apple.com/jp/book/dagger-light-at-end-world/id967516696?mt=11

Easy, right? This way, Amazon will see that your book is free wherever you like. Don't send all these links in a single mail, I suggest. Sometimes they will put it permafree on every store, sometimes only in the English language ones (.com .uk .ca .au). See how it goes and then provide them with the japanese and brazilian links.

You'll get an answer by Amazon in a day or two, usually, and they will set your book permafree. Don't worry if it will take a couple of days for your new price to show on your product page, sometimes it happens.

Now you have a permafree book you can use to draw attention to all the other books that you're selling. Usually, for every 100 copies of Dagger 1 people download, they will buy 10 of Dagger 2, which I sell at 2,99. With three upcoming chapters and a whole life of books I still have to write, you probably see where I'm getting at: free is worth your time. Free is beautiful. You give people what they want, you say *Have a taste, my friend. Be my guest* and they will come for more. And more.

This is why I'm a huge permafree fan, but if you're not, it's okay. Amazon has a wonderful option that is called *kdp select*. Every 90 days, you can choose 5 days of free promotions, or discounted price, and I do suggest you use this.

You can even decide to have your book permafree just for a couple of years, let's say, or some months. What do you have to gain? Eheh. Everything.

Giving away a product for free will surely allow you to get more reviews (positively, *good* reviews) and as we said before, reviews have a great, GREAT importance in you Amazon search results and consequent rankings.

If you have a permafree book, of course, you're not allowed to use KDP select, which allows you to draw traffic from the members who subscribed to the program (it has a lot of advantages, you can read all about it here: https://kdp.amazon.com/select). If you have a book on kdp, you will have a share of the total amount of KDP select money divided by the pages of your book that people have read. This is a good and fair way to divide the shares. Once they used to pay you per *copy*, and that was really deleterious for people like me who writes LONG, fantasy books (I used to get half of the regular royalties for a book sold via KDP select), since a 30 pages short story was paid just like a long saga. Now royalties are divided by page I earn MORE with a copy sold via KDP that a ordinarily sold one. My book 1 of course is free and this means it's available on other stores and therefore can't be eligible for KDP select. But I put book 2 and the others with KDP to earn more and it's working.

Of course, with the present royalties-per-page system you earn more if you write longer books. You don't have to stretch your book just because of this, BUT, inserting extra content at the end of you book will probably end up in more money for you (extra note\comment from the author; deleted scenes; mail correspondence with your editors and so on).

So remember: sold the other books' weight in gold, but set one book permafree to draw traffic and reviews.

This brings us to the next argument we're going to cover: reviews.

Way more important that you can possibly think.

REVIEWS

Reviews are important, but why? Because Amazon likes to sell good products, and reviews are the only way Amazon can get social proof that your book is good. We all think we wrote the best novel of all times; writers *work* like this. Our book is the best one, of course, but Amazon has a problem: there are MILLIONS of *best books ever* in her breast (I like to think of Amazon as a woman, you see). So which one deserves to show higher?

You're right, fellows: the ones with more positive reviews. Search, again, for an important keyword like *fantasy*, or *horror books*, or whatever; something with a lot of search results in it. Whatever you wrote, the books showing higher surely have something like THOUSANDS of reviews, and surely they have a 4 or 4.5 (if not five) average (the five orange stars we all know).

What does this mean? You have to get reviews. Simple. You don't have to be afraid about what people think about your book, because with time this will lead you to make even more money.

The problem is that people don't like to waste their time writing a review, even if they loved the book. I know from personal experience: if everyone who loved the first book of

Dagger had left a review, at this time I would have thousands of reviews. No kidding: I just need to see how many people bought the following books, and I do hope you have loved the first book if you spend 2.99 bucks to know how the story goes on.

Reviews take time. People are afraid to write stupid things. People forget. I don't know. I don't know why a very low percentage of people who read a book leave a review, if not asked to: no more than 3%, and not all of them may be good. But, let's say, this *may* happen because after you have finished a book, you have to go on Amazon, search for the book, click-click a thousand times and then leave a review trying to sound intelligent. People have to much to do in their lives to do something like this.

Save their time! There's a great thing we can do to gain more reviews: ask for them. Be it fiction or non fiction, if a reader gets to the bottom of your book he\she probably enjoyed it, so he\she will be more kind to you and write a positive review. We want to make her life easier and save her time, so we can write something like this: *Did you enjoy the book? Please leave a review. You can do it at the following link:* HTTP://www.amazon.com/review/create-review?-ie=UTF8&asin=B00KTR8C90

Yes, my dear warriors: you must provide the *review* link!

Write the URL of your comment page as a hyperlink, just like I showed (that's my *Dagger write a review* page). Use this exact link, just like it's written, only changing the ASIN with the one of your book (the last 10 characters).

You're asking it kindly, so probably readers will do it. Still, not all of them, of course, because some of them are really lazy. But surely more than 3%.

By the way, tell them they can even write a short one.

This way you will surely raise your positive reviews, and you can easily understand why: if a reader has got to the end of your book (where you write *leave a review*) it's more than probable that he liked it and will leave a positive review. If I hate a book, especially a free one, I don't get to the end where somebody is asking me to write a review.

If you do this at an early stage of your career, with months, with years, you'll get the hundreds or thousands of reviews you need. This works best with a permafree book, but it will work all the same with kdp select days and with pay books.

Again, if you wrote a book full of typos, badly edited, a story full of plot-holes, you may get bad reviews and a two or three stars rated book will show poorly on Amazon search results.

This was just a tip. People love to be *asked about what they think about things*. They like to give an opinion. I'm not a huge goodreads.com fan, but without any doubt there are a lot of groups where to share your book and ask for a honest review.

You got a negative review? Don't be mad at people. Amazon is funded on the honest opinions of people. Amazon itself reminds you, though, that you and your faithful readers can mark any review as *useful* or *useless*, and this will bring it down or up. This is a good way to decrease the importance of a fake review, be it good or bad, be it about our book or someone else's. Of course you will one day get negative reviews and some of them may even be right. Don't be mad for it. Scroll Stephen King's books, or Martin's, or Tolkien's, they DO get negative reviews too, and you know what? That's good, it gives the system credibility. And it will give credibility to your book, too. Why? You can guess why: I'll never buy a book with only 200, or even 20, five stars reviews. It smells of cheating. I like, for instance 15 five stars, 8 four stars, 5 three stars, 3 two stars and 1 one stars reviews. Believe me, this is the look you want for your reviews diagram. Bad reviews (well, a little of them) are so important that if your book is so good not to get some, you should write one yourself.

I'm joking, don't do it, it was just to give you an idea.

A little bird told me that useful reviews have a higher importance to Amazon algorithm.

Now.

SUPER TIP about reviews

One thing that really worked for me is scrolling the Amazon.com list of top 1000 reviewers. Every Amazon user is a reviewer, so there are hundreds of millions of us. Some of them really care to get into the top 1000, or top 100. You know, there's a sort of struggle for survival among them, most of them write something like four or five reviews everyday and are always looking for new material. You know what this means? Of course: gold! Shining bucks!

A reviewer shows higher on the list not only depending on the total number of reviews he or she has written, but also depending on the *useful review* vote he gets from Amazon users. This, in my humble opinion, lead most of them to write only good reviews, that your readers will eventually like and mark as useful reviews.

Go to the list, that is here:

http://www.amazon.com/review/top-reviewers

Most of them leave an e-mail where to be contacted. They'll like to hear from you, so leave them a message. Not to all of them, mind you. Take a quick look at what they've reviewed in the past;

some may review only dvds, or pc-games, or electronics. Save your time (and their time) by looking for reviewers that will do, you've got thousand of names after all.

You'll be sending something like hundreds of e-mail, so it's better you create a template that you will send to everyone, changing only their names (people like to be called by name, so don't be cold). Something like this will do: *Good morning, Alex. I'm CJ, I wrote this, I'd be honored to get your honest review about this: (link to your book page). I would put it in my editorial reviews section. Warmly, CJ.*

Be short and efficient. Not all of them will review your book. Not all of them will actually answer to your mail. But this simple trick lead me to have this wonderful review by one of the best reviewers in the world: http://www.amazon.com/review/R3DQ5BN1QTHE3K/ref=cm_cr_rdp_perm?ie=UTF8&ASIN=B00KTR8C90

As you can see, I used my author central profile to get this review into the *editorial reviews section*, that is very useful since it brings your best reviews on the top of your page, without people having to look for them through hundreds of reviews.

As before: be creative. You can ask everyone for a review, but mind: Amazon has recently sued people who were *selling* their reviews on the net, so avoid web services asking money for reviews (there are still some). Amazon will find it out, sooner or later, erasing that review from the site and you will have wasted your money. With time, this will even give you problems with them, so be careful.

Another easy way to get more reviews is simply googling *your genre + reviews* (horror reviews, fantasy reviews, erotica reviews, science fiction reviews and so on). Google will show you the sites\forums where you can possibly find reviewers interested in reviewing your book on their sites, blogs, forums or whatever. Mind: our aim is to get more reviews on *Amazon*. One review on Amazon has more power than a review posted on a small blog, so remember to kindly ask your reviewers to post their reviews on Amazon too. Don't use flattery with them but remember to be kind; these people are giving you the most important thing they have: their time. Just like readers.

Once I wrote about 200 hundred e-mails in a *day* to Amazon reviewers. This can be tiring, so you can start slowly and write about 5 or 10 e-mails everyday and see what happens.

There's twitter, facebook, reading groups. You can have a contest, with a prize for the best review you get in a given time, and make it a facebook event.

Be creative.

Reviews are important.

DRAW TRAFFIC

We said before that the price of your book has an importance too, for your Amazon search results rankings. Your book will show higher if you set its price at 2.99 instead of 0.99. And of course 10.99 will show even higher. What's the problem with this? That no one will buy your book at 10.99. Two readers will buy it at 2.99 and ten, or twenty will buy it at 0.99. A hundred, in my case, will download my book if it is free, and the copies you sell have their importance, too.

After all these years, I still don't understand why some writers set their books' price permanently to 0.99; this price, in my humble opinion has all the cons of a permanently free book (0.99 is the new free, it means *cheap*) and the cons of a pay book (readers has to pay for it *anyway*, this means that it's not really free, you know). It can be a good price for a promotion, for a limited period of time thanks to kdp select days, but setting your book price permanently to 0.99 is some kind of slow suicide. Make strong decisions: free or pay, no middle way. 0.99 gives you more or less 0.30 cents of royalties per copy. If you use this price just to have a wider audience and to be paid at the same time, use the permafree option and sell your other books at a better price. Better results guaranteed.

If you think I'm wrong, it's okay. Look at your sales page: that will never lie, and will always tell you the truth. Experiment a little and see what works best.

You have to find your way, your equilibrium I dare say. What I want you to understand is that there's no easy way: Amazon algorithm is complex and includes a lot of factors, as we have seen. The only thing we can do is try, and try again.

This is why I think it's important to draw traffic to your book page from outside Amazon. You can't rely on Amazon alone, even if we all agree that Amazon does a lot of work for us and has made our life easier. It sends mail, you may have noticed, to people suggesting our book. That's great. So let's say that you have to help Amazon, too.

How? Using twitter, facebook, mailing lists, your personal website and so on.

I'm not a great fan of twitter, so I won't water down my book writing about something that I don't know. Why? Because I want to get back to Dagger as soon as I can and because there are a lot of ebooks out there, telling you how to use twitter. I prefer facebook. I'm a facebook fan, and again I don't get money by Zuckerberg for saying this.

I like this list by Shelley Hitz:

http://www.trainingauthors.com/facebook-groups-for-authors/

I suggest you join the groups and post about your book once a day. You can do it even without a pilot poster (it will take just 5 minutes of your precious time) and will draw traffic to your book. How do I know? Why am I so sure about it? Because I made experiments, that's why. Join the amazon affiliate program on: https://affiliate-program.amazon.com/, and learn all about it. Not only it will give you some more royalties, if used correctly, but will provide you with some more data. Using an affiliate link I realized that my affiliate downloads were raising sensibly on the days I promoted on facebook groups, so that's a certainty.

Then, if you can't still afford a website (I know, high costs-low benefits in the short time is never good) create at least a facebook page about you (as a author, not about your book, that will have to come later) and put the link at the end of your book. Have readers contact you via your facebook page. If you ask them to *follow* you, after the have just liked the page, you will have an easier sort of mailing list.

One tactic that really worked for me is the use and promotion of the **facebook button**. What is it? When you create a facebook page and reach a tot followers, you will get a button on your page, which, if clicked, will lead the visitor to the product page or to any other http link you chose. So you can link your Amazon ebook page directly here. As you can imagine, there's not going to be an army of people clicking on it.

But you can promote it! The main error with the use of facebook promotions is that people promote their pages instead of this wonderful tool that Facebook gives us. You don't want just to get *likes*. You want to get readers and for that you have to promote the link in your button. That may sound bad, but listen to me.

You go on your facebook button and select, 'Help people find out more'. Click. Now you can set up your facebook promotion that will lead DIRECTLY to your amazon product page. Less passages, more chances to sell.

There are a lot of walkthroughs on the net provided to help you to set a facebook promotions. My suggestion is: choose both sexes and set 'Amazon kindle' as main interest of your target audience. This way you may be sure that the target of this promotion is a kindle reader. As second interest, select something related to your genre. (Stephen King, Vampires, Twin Peaks, whatever.) Experiment some and watch the result. You may have to waste a couple of bucks before you realize how to make it work.

SUPER IMPORTANT TIP!

Remember when I told you how to put a keyword in the link of your product page? Do it here. Please do. The link in your facebook button must contain a keyword, you decide which one. If used properly, this little tip may have your book really skyrocket, and generate more sales. Of course this is not a free method, it's called advertising. But I wrote it: sooner or later you will have to spend money to get money, just like with mailing list services.

Grow a fan base and focus on you author platform. You can't build a pyramid starting from the top, right? If the Roman Empire lasted so long is partly because Roman cities had a great sewer system.

If someone writes an unreadable book and think he can climb Amazon's charts with a couple of tricks, he's just building pyramids starting from their tops. Don't do that.

Write a good book. Grow a fan base. Advertise.

Let's talk about the fan base thing. I think there's a lot of potential in the last part of your book, that not everybody is using: the thanks page. You thank the people who helped you writing the book, you thank your readers and so on, a bit like the academy awards ceremony, you know? *I want to thank my producer, my god and my mom and so on.*

Be funny, keep the reader's attention alive and then write something like this: *come to facebook and tell me you liked the book\you can send your marriage proposal at my personal e-mail: aaaaaaa@aaa.com*

People like to get involved, and to laugh. They like to be asked about what they think. I spend some minutes everyday answering to my readers. Some of my readers have, with time, even become my friends. They will think you're a nice person (not like all those other writers who think they are Charles Dickens) and they will come for more. This means gold, okay, but this means making your life, and their lives, better. This is why we write. I like people.

I dare say, this is a pretty southern-european way of thinking, that I'm trying to export in the US. Don't be to formal, don't be cold. No one likes cold people, this is why we loved Chaplin and Robin Williams.

Know the name of your readers' dogs; ask what they do in their lives. Of course, you won't be able to do it when you'll have millions of readers, but until you have *that* problem I suggest to be very informal. Don't just get their mail to spam, we're sick with that.

Most of your readers will prefer to stay in the dark. It's okay. Talk to the ones who will show up, because people will talk to people, who will talk to people. Yes: I'm building my pyramid starting from its base. It takes time, of course (in my experience, it takes *years*), but it's the best advertising you can hope for. It's a social web way more powerful than internet once it grows. Revolutions started like this in the past.

On your facebook page, write about your books once in a while, or about the one you're writing now. This worked like hell for me and I think this had a great importance in making Dagger the MOST downloaded fantasy in Italy in 2015 (of course, not the most read or the most bought, not in the US or UK, I know, but still the most downloaded fantasy book in my country).

If you're a twitter user, even better.

Now. A lot of Amazon gurus are saying that mailing list have a great importance, too. I agree with them, especially if you're writing a saga or a series of book: you'd better begin as soon as possible to have one. You will use it to tell your faithful readers when you're next book is coming up, so that they don't have to search for it on Amazon every week. I use mailchimp. It takes no time no sign up, and it's free up to 2000 contacts.

Some writers offer a free gift for users signing up to their mailing list.

That sounds like a good idea, but everyone is doing it and readers now understand it's a trick.

I prefer my *Flag Ship Theory*.

THE FLAG SHIP THEORY

Choose one of your books as a flag ship to advertise all the others. Now, if you have a permafree book everything is easier, but you can do it even with a pay book. At the end of the novel, or marketing guide for what I know, put a link to your other books or the following novel. Save people their time. If you've got the book 2 of a series, put a link at the end of book 1, so people can buy it as soon as they want and don't have to look for it.

You want to do something special? Put the cover image of your next book to draw more attention as soon as possible.

Now you know why the ending of Dagger 1 looks like this:

(...) Reviews are important; you can help me by writing even a short one at the following link: http://tinyurl.com/dagger1review. It will help people find Dagger (or avoid it!).

The saga continues with 'Dagger 2–Blood Brothers', now available on Amazon:

www.amazon.com/gp/product/B00UGJGLSA

I hope to see you again, otherwise it was a pleasure to meet you.

That's all folks.

Good night.

Stay tuned. Join Dagger newsletter: http://eepurl.com/bMjYC5

Here we are again. This is how I think every book should end: 1) thank you readers, see you on Monday. 2) hey, by the way, write a review if you've got the time. 3) I forgot, the next book is this and you can find it here 4) this is the cover image, by the way. 5) Ha! If you want to stay tuned about Dagger you can sign up for my free mailing list.

And that's the end of it.

Be nice, smart, don't look nervous. People will love you.

Of course you can put as many links as you want in your book's ending, but try to be clever: you don't want people to run away from you, right, so don't fill it up too much.

If you have a series, or a pentalogy, you don't need to put the links to all your books at the end of book one; just to book two. You can put the link to book three directly at the end of book two, and so on.

Cover Image

I will talk shortly about this but it does have a lot of importance. The cover image of your book is probably the first thing a reader is going to notice. Then comes the title. Then the author name. Then they will click and read the book description. Then they will or won't buy. And we want them to buy, of course, because we could spend our youth drinking wine, playing videogames and driving fast cars, instead we've spent the best years of our lives writing books and now we want the world and we want it now.

So let's get back to point one: your cover image. I've already written that a cover image MUST look professional. There's no other way. You can't help it. Some artists will ask 2000 dollars, some 50. Results may vary and of course keep an eye on your wallet, but I'm afraid that you have to spend some bucks if you want to get where the real money are made.

Yes, yes, Walt, we all know this.

Okay. So let's move to the next step: which cover images will CATCH the sight of your potential readers?

I will talk about two different things here: *chromatic vector*, and *sexual vector*.

Chromatic vector: remember that we're animals. No. I'm not going mad. We're basically animals and our brains work like that. We see some colors and we instinctively react in some way, because when we were in the mother forest our brain was looking for colorful fruits and felt sure at the red light of a fire burning in the night. We were afraid to see our red blood because our body knew this could mean death, and our eyes reacted to bright colors because we knew that poisonous snakes or spiders were bright orange, red or yellow.

Are you following me? Yes? Good. You're not following me? I will explain. We react instinctively when we see a bright color on a black surface, more than when we see, let's say, beige on gray.

So you probably want to use a bright orange writing on black background, with fire raising everywhere and a monster coming out of the fire for your book.

Like this.

Whenever I take a look at Dagger in my Amazon rankings, I always notice how it really comes out of the screen, compared to what's around it.

I always suggest orange on black, this is why the cover of this book itself is basically orange writings on a black background. I love Lamborghini cars and hope that I can afford one, one day. I love it painted orange, you see, with black windows at night. Nobody notices a gray Lamborghini so make your book a beautiful, orange Lamborghini Murcielago. It's the best tip I can give you on the matter. Tastes vary, of course, but readers eyes don't.

Let's talk about the other one, the sexual vector: I think you already know what I'm talking about here, so I'll make it short. Yes. We are animals and *yes*, we need to reproduce ourselves for the continuation of the specie, so every time we're put in front of a pertinent sexual image our attention is drawn and our mind goes BLING BLING!

You can see it everywhere: sexual (more or less explicit) images are proliferating throughout Amazon. In the fantasy rankings themselves you'll find a lot of, well, boobs next to the lord of the rings. I think that people are actually making a wrong use of this and soon we'll find ourselves surrounded by boobs. Okay, I agree, it's not *that* problem after all, if we think about it, but this is not the trick that I'm using. There are a lot of sexually explicit scenes in Dagger but I don't feel like using a sexual vector in my book cover.

Sexual vectors work good, of course, with romance books and erotic books; may work fine with thrillers if there's a femme fatale in them, for instance. Just try to stick to the book: if it has some connection with your plot, take in consideration the possibility to use a sexual vector. If you're writing a book marketing guide, it's better you don't. It's better you use orange writings on plain black background.

Why vectors are important? Anyway, why is it important to have a book cover that draws attention as soon as possible? Because you may not rank #1 in a search result, BUT, on a pc screen you visualize the first five Amazon search results, and people will see our orange book cover (or the boobs) first even if you rank nr #5 (Bite the dust, number 1!).

This is why I decided to talk briefly about this. It doesn't matter for us to get to number one in a search result, we just need to get on the first page, as long as we have a cover image that kicks.

Different stores, different rules.

Amazon.com is the biggest Amazon store both for traffic and number of books. There are other 12 Amazon stores, however, that can generate independent traffic and income to your books. They work pretty similarly, but there are a lot of differences between them.

First of all, remember the importance of authorcentral, the service that Amazon offers you to personalize your author page, link your books between them, show your pictures and coming events. Look at any book on Amazon (let's say, the *important* ones); below the book's ranking you'll see the *More about the author* section, showing a little bio and the author's picture. Click on it and *bingo*, a costumer will get all the info he\she needs about you and your books.

Most indie authors don't personalize their authorcentral page (I heard about 70%) and that is a great mistake. People want to know about us—about their favorite writers, right? So do that and you'll be ahead of 70% of indies out there.

One thing that even pro Amazon authors sometimes forget is that every store has its own authorcentral page and profile. This means that if you personalize your authorcentral.com profile and have a great author page on amazon.com, that won't show up on all the other stores (amazon.uk, for instance, that is a HUGE store).

So remember to sign in even on https://authorcentral.amazon.co.uk (United Kingdom); https://authorcentral.amazon.de/ (Germany); https://authorcentral.amazon.fr/ (France). The Japanese one is good only for printed books. The other stores, at the moment, don't have their relative authorcentral service and I hope Amazon fixes that sooner or later.

Now. Different prices work differently with different stores. What does this mean? Take Amazon.in, Amazon store in India. India is a fast growing market and I do suggest you grasp all the possibilities it can offer. The *problem* (or the beautiful side, it depends on the point of view) of India is that books are cheap, very cheap. You can buy a paperback for a dollar or two, and I don't mean the second-hand ones, but new, shiny books just printed. So your 2.99 dollars ebook that sells good on Amazon.com and uk may sell nothing in India or Mexico. Amazon knows this, of course, and gives you the chance to select different prices for different stores. In India, I sell the second book of Dagger at 99 rupees, something like our 0.99 (mind: I'm using this price only in these cases). Do the same even with Mexico and Brazil. I know, if people can buy an ebook reader they probably have enough money for our book, too. It's just that they have new paperback at 99 rupees, too.

How can we maximize our income on smaller stores like .de or .fr, where people have a fair knowledge of English? You can create a 'French' or 'German' version of your book. This doesn't mean to translate your book in that language. The book you're selling is pretty much the same (you can add a personalized introduction for your french or german audience, of course) but it has another ASIN. It's a different book and I give you three seconds to tell me what does this mean, or better, what is the use of having another version of your book to use only on those stores.

...

Of course. 350 more characters to spend in keywords. And of course you're going to use *french* or *german* keywords (fantasy livre anglais, novelle cusine tres jolie le jeux sont fait!). Don't translate the books—we'll talk about that in a few minutes—translate the keywords! Of course be careful not to make two versions of the same book available on the same stores. Remember you can opt in or out all the nations in this world on the second page of your book publishing process on kdp (I love Amazon, it *does* think about everything). Use the *German* version of your *English* book in all the German speaking countries and you'll see your sales and downloads grow.

Be careful to create the alternative version of your book only *after* you have linked your books 1, 2, and 3, if we are talking about a saga. It may be that Amazon will link your English book 1 with your German book 2, and then you will have to contact Amazon to fix the mistake (it happened to me).

This little trick won't give you tons of copies, I'm honest about that, but surely it will increase your rankings on minor stores and will do it forever. Remember that 10 dollars every month on Amazon.de is 110 dollars every year, possibly for all your life. And you can add to that the 10 dollars per month you earn in France, why not... what I mean is *take no prisoners*, and seize all the opportunities. Small incomes become great with time.

Amazon.it is a growing market and there can be some chances even for English books (I have to confess that sometimes I sell the English version of my book in Italy, and sometimes the Italian one on the other stores, so be careful to made ALL your books available EVERYWHERE, even if it won't sell millions of copies). One crazy law in Italy concerns ebooks: if you have an ISBN, the IVA (that is to say the national tax) is 5%, that is way lower than the English and German ones, for instance. BUT. If you don't have an ISBN and you have just an ASIN (what all our books have) you pay 23% of IVA! Of course, I totally agree that is crazy. It's not a sequence of numbers or letters to make a book, but if you're planning to sell your ebooks in Italy, providing your book with a ISBN is something you have to consider.

Having your book translated into another language will always make you look more professional and stand out as an author. Imagine people taking a look at your author page and seeing your book in different languages. It's what I'd expect from Wilbur Smith or Stephen King, right? Of course, I know what you're thinking about: translations are *expensive*. Yes, they are. And this is not the only problem with them: you don't have control on your book once it's written in a language you don't understand. You have to find someone you trust, and you now how hard that can be.

This is why I translated my books in English by myself and then had them edited and copyedited by professional editors.

I have to admit, though, that I'd be in trouble if I wanted a German version of Dagger. At the moment I'm pretty good with my English and Italian markets and I'm putting all my efforts in them. Financing a Spanish translation is one of my goals and sooner or later I'll do it, but it's an investment that I have no intention to make now.

There is, anyhow, a quick way to have your books translated in a LOT of languages and that is: http://www.babelcube.com/ give it a look and read how it works.

I must say I never used it and I have to admit that I'm not totally happy with the idea of giving up a part of my royalties to the translator. My idea of coworking is different: I pay you for a service (editing, book cover and so on), I pay you even some thousand bucks, but that's the end of that. We sign a contract in which we both states to be happy with this method and farewell. Having to share forever your book or one of his versions with someone doesn't, let's say, put me at ease.

But Babelcube is an option you may consider for small markets, or if you want a quick way to have your book speak italiano or deutsch!

Mailing lists

We said it's important to grow our own mailing list to keep our readers informed about what we do over the years. The sooner you begin to create it, the better.

There are, anyway, a lot of mailing lists services out there on the internet. These services will send the link to your book to THEIR email subscribers. They may do it for free or have you pay a fee. They may millions of subscribers or just 4.000. They may accept everyone or be very selective.

But their usefulness is beyond any doubt. It's easy to see if they work or not just watching your sales diagram on your kdp profile the day they send your book to their subscribers.

Of course, the most efficient ones are the most expensive (like everything in life) so my suggestion is to avoid random promotions and to plan in details, months before, what you will do.

Remember: you don't have dreams. You have goals. A goal without a plan, is just a dream.

There are a lot of services. I provide this list, but there may be others: http://www.indiesunlimited.com/book-promo-sites/ a quick look on Google and you will find them all.

I can't talk to you about all of them, because I haven't tried all of them. I tried http://buckbooks.net/ (one of the youngest services out there). It gave me more or less 250 additional free book downloads for Dagger 1. That was a pretty good result for what I paid. For prices, I'm sorry, you have to talk with them.

We know that https://www.bookbub.com/ has been for years the best service, and probably it still is. It's expensive, this is probably due to the fact that it actually works. They have MILLIONS of subscribers, divided by genres. They are very selective though and reject the 80% of the proposals. They are now accepting even permafree books, though, so anyway give it a try. I suggest you sign up with them and upload all the data of your books. Not only that makes your submission easier (and with more chance to be accepted, in my humble opinion), but even if you are rejected your book will still show up on their website, giving you a little more exposure.

You must take any chance to have your book show up *anywhere*. If a blog has no more than 20 visitors every month, it still has 240 every year. If you get 240 people see your book every year in 10 or 20 different blogs that will be 2400 and 4800 visitors per year, so think about it.

Another suggestion: if you use all the mailing list services together, you'll never know which one is working and which, on the other hand, is just wasting your money and time. Try one of them once a week, or month. Try them separately to see if they work or not. THEN. Make a plan and use them altogether on a single day (I suggest a Sunday, when people take a break from work and buy something to read in their free time). This will have a cumulative effect that will last for days, and maybe bring your kdp sales chart permanently on a higher level.

The more you sell, the more you sell. Simple as that: climbing Amazon rankings will tell Amazon that your book is doing good, and Amazon itself will help you sell your book. Reinforcement, remember?

The ranking of a book will, in fact, bring it higher and higher on the Amazon search results, giving you a wider audience.

Now. I can't remember how many times I spent entire days sending my requests to the mailing lists websites, asking them to promote my book on a given day to their subscribers. It takes a lot of time, and we need time, right? We need it to write, edit and give the world better books.

Sooner or later there comes a time when you have to give yourself over to automation, on such minor tasks, because it's not possible to do everything by ourselves.

Nowadays, some software come in handy when you have to send your requests to free mailing lists sites (as the ones listed above) to promote your book or books. Given you have a book you wish to promote under the regular price with your kdp select days (or free, or *permafree*), these software will send the relative request to *dozens* of mailing lists sites. They will do, in less than a minute, what usually takes hours of our precious time. **Automation**, that's right. It will save you about an afternoon getting tired in front of a pc screen.

I'll talk about the two that I know better; both have vantages and disadvantages:

KDroi is one of the most used worldwide and you can find it here: http://www.kdroi.com/ (once again, I don't get money from them). At the time the present book is written, it can send your book promotion request to 32 free mailing lists total, but there are restrictions for .99 and permafree books—that just means you have less choice, because not all mailing lists accept the same things, and KDroi will automatically select them depending on the case, saving you the time and the effort to read ALL their terms and conditions, too.

What I love about this service is that it's insanely cheap compared to similar software and it's a **one time payment**. You pay once, and you can use it for a lifetime (just like Kindle Samurai). You'll get regular updates every time KDroi producers will add another mailing list to their portfolio. So maybe when you're reading this book they will have some more than 32. In addiction to this, it's a web browser extension, this means it's very easy to use both with Firefox and Google Chrome.

You can plan your promos months in advance, which I suggest, automating in a couple of minutes a work that otherwise would take you days…and you can use that time to write more books and sell more. I repeat: we don't have all the time in the world. Save time. Automate what you can: editing, promotions, mailing lists, people taking care of your books. The more money you get, the more you can invest in making more and quicker money!

For other software similar to KDroi you have to pay a fee every month, and this is the case of **K Optimizer**, another great help that you can find here: http://www.koptimizer.com/. You're right. It's going to cost you more and it's going to cost you something every month, but it has a lot of features. It has, at the moment, 63 free websites where you can send your promos for consideration—30+ mailing lists, like KDroi, and 30+ free press release websites.

One of its best features is the possibility to chose one of your keywords as a main keyword to rank higher. So if you want to rank higher in, let's say, *super high fantasy kindle books*, you type that on the keywords window and K Optimizer will help you rank higher for *that*, too (remember when I told you how the URL of your ebook can have the keyword inside it? Well, they put it to good use). Talking to you about how to rank higher with a determined keyword is why I decided to write this book, this is why I consider this a great feature.

K Optimizer will also help you to keep track of your promotions, and *allows you to easily track and manage all of your Kindle books in one place by providing your books keyword ranking* (as its written on their website. I add: information = money. Automation = time = even more money) sending you alerts when you can do a new KDP promotion, when your ranks are falling down, and other significant happenings.

You pay more, you get more. Simple as that. I know money is an important matter we all have to consider, especially when we're moving the first steps as writers and/or we don't have a lot of money to invest.

As I said, there's nothing these software do that you can't do manually, (apart from merchantwords.com, since we don't know the data it provides). What Kindle Samurai does, you can do it on your own, but typing every keyword on the Amazon search bar and scrolling the results, trying to figure out if the keywords show up in the books' title and description too, takes DAYS, a lot of time, and you can easily miss information. Kindle Samurai does it in a few seconds. Automation with mailing list websites works just the same.

This being said, you can begin sending requests manually, then move to KDroi (as you make more money) then move to K Optimizer (as you make even more money).

The more you gain, the more you invest.

The more you invest, the more you gain.

That's the whole story.

One last tip: it's better to do 100 things on a single day, than 1 thing on 100 days. Concentrate your efforts, all your efforts, on a single day. Plan months in advance, have a strategy. To conquer Iwo Jima don't send there one ship at a time, but use all your troops and guns in a single attack.

My suggestion for a good plan is this: first work on your book. No typos, a good editing and a good cover image, a compelling story, if you write fiction, and so on.

Then work on your book page as described in this book, to both look professional and show higher in search results, twisting with the keywords as suggested.

Then work on your reviews. You have to get reviews somehow, you can't escape from them. Reviews bring readers. Readers bring reviews, and so on.

Then work on advertising. Money are made with money, this is crystal clear. You know the guys in the top 100? They spend money to make money and we want to be in their company as soon as possible to get our Lamborghini.

When you find something that works, do it and do it again.

But, most of all

STUDY!

Keep yourself informed. Talk with people in your field or similar fields, attend webinars and read writing and marketing blogs. Gather knowledge and share it.

There are a lot of sites that once in a while inform you about discounts on marketing products or give them away for free. One of the best ones I'm aware of is http://goodriter.com/ It was born recently, on 2015. Sign up, it's totally free and you can unregister whenever you want.

You will get a free video training even here: http://www.yourfirst10kreaders.com/ this is the site where I learned the basics about keywords, which I developed afterwards.

It's a good starting point for beginners and even some pros may have something to learn.

I love http://kindlepreneur.com/ too, not only for its wonderful graphic and artworks, but because it sticks to the point and doesn't waste words, a bit like me.

Spend a buck or two in kdp manuals and ebooks, there are a lot on Amazon itself, but beware: there are a lot of people, too, who are making a living telling nothing, really nothing, because they have learned how to sell fried air. I could give you a couple of names, but that would be unfair. They are the reasons why I decided to write this.

Write better books, sell them better. I've got a feeling that sooner or later this *kindle gold rush*, as someone has already named it, will come to an end. So we have to get the best of it in the shortest time possible. This means you have to get and maintain a fair knowledge of the market and its rules, so keep updated.

Now. I think there's very little I could add. Amazon has its rules, a lot of rules, but it surely is one of the best possibilities for us authors out there on the web. Just some years ago our life was harder: we had to prostrate ourselves at the feet of editors in the hope to get a chance to be published, getting virtually no royalties if you weren't really (I mean, *really*) lucky.

Amazon has made its revolution: it has changed the way people reads books. It has changed the way *we* write books.

Everyone of us is given a chance, and thanks to kdp we all start from the same point. It's a long run and you'll get nowhere if you don't learn how to run faster than everybody else.

The key to success is to try and try and try until you find the right combination, the recipe that works for you and no one else.

I've found mine and wrote this book to let you know, and to help you if I can. If you have suggestions, if you have doubts, I give you my email address: waltpopester@yahoo.com

I'm new to this and I need all the help possible. It isn't actually my field, but I recently received a lot of appreciation for putting all this info in one little, tight and cheap handbook. By now you should know how important reviews are, so please write even a short one at the following link: http://tinyurl.com/EbooksMarketingReviews.

I'd appreciate your friendship on facebook. Tell me your experience, your difficulties, let's talk for a while. Sharing knowledge is one of the best ways to become better sellers, better writers, better persons.

I'll frequently publish updates for this project. Please join my mailing list where I'll write you whenever a new version of the handbook is available. No spam policy guaranteed: http://eepurl.com/b0EKJ1.

By the way, there's two little extra gifts for you on the next pages.

That's all folks.

Good night.

- (This is a little article I wrote in 2016 about international markets and their infinite potentials. You may already know some of the tips and info given, so you'll find it easy to read.)

Selling Books Internationally: Why You Should Consider it

We all would like to be an Amazon.com best-seller. The thing is, there are 4.7 millions of books out there who are, more or less, struggling for our same purpose; too much traffic, and you know how hard it becomes to put your head out of the waterline, even following all the advice our kdp *coaches* are giving us.

Focusing on keywords with high traffic and low competition is fundamental, but what not everybody knows is that it's true even for choosing the market where to sell your books. This is why I'm writing about my little experience as an *international* indie author.

In this article, we'll discuss:

- Why you should consider focusing internationally
- How to get your book translated

- Tips on how to optimize for foreign markets

- **Why Work to Sell Internationally?**

Because the world is big and there's a special place for everyone, even for you. This may be the moral teaching of some fantasy book… but it's true for marketing, too! I call those special places *the little ponds*.

Hey, what are you talking about? What are the little ponds? you ask. Well, Amazon has 13 markets all around the world (the ones where you usually earn something like 1.99 dollars every month, just because some expatriate found your book, maybe). All those *.es .fr .de .something* – *those* are the small ponds, and there you can be a fish as big as you want, my friend. You just need to do the right things, and I'm here to help you with that.

Believe me. Smaller markets give you a bigger chance to end up in their top 100, and I don't mean the top 100 *something* (top 100 Kindle ebooks\Fantasy\Dark fantasy\Dark fantasy that my aunt would read on a Sunday morning when she is bored), like it happens on the .com. I mean top 100 *general*. The real top 100, the one where everybody wishes to be.

- **What Do We, THE WRITERS, Have to Gain?**

Dollars. Bucks. You know, they are usually round and when they bounce against each other they sound *din din*. If we're here it's because we mean business, right? So let's begin with something that's very familiar to you. Royalties schemes. This is mine:

No, there's nothing wrong in my Amazon profile. One of those places where you usually earn the famous 1.99 per month is actually my dreamland.

In a market as little as Amazon.it I'm selling more than *.com* and *.uk* put together. Strange, isn't it? The whole truth: a third of the money I earn comes from Kindle Unlimited, which can't be visualized in that scheme, but the royalties I get from KU follow the same proportions.

Okay, being Italian, in the beginning I focused my attention on the Italian market and that wasn't *totally* a choice (it's just that I had an *Italian* book, you know). I had my ups and downs, like everybody. I followed the permafree technique, that is to say: put the first book of your saga permanently free and then sell the following episodes their worth in gold (2.99 euros\dollars, which is much in this 0.99 world). I studied a lot, of course, and mastered the use (I'd rather say the art) of keywords by attending webinars and reading marketing courses like everybody, and when I made the right choices my sales diagram skyrocketed to the heavens. In the end I managed to gain a dominating presence on my slice of market and become one of the most popular fantasy writer in my country. Cool, isn't it? Would that have ever happened on the *.com*? Of course not. At least, not so soon.

Since three years the first (Italian) book of my saga, 'Dagger – La Luce alla Fine del Mondo' is permanently in the top 100 general of Amazon.it (the free one), and always somewhere between #1 and #6 most downloaded fantasy. I'll offer no screenshot. Just look the ranking of the book right now, whenever you are reading this little article: http://tinyurl.com/Dagger1Italian.

Of course, the more people download the first book, the more copies I sell of the following installments.

Then I had my books translated in English, had them edited by a professional editor, and I had the same kick-ass cover art.

What happened? For some kind of reason I wasn't getting the same results in terms of sold copies. You know that sensation, right? Struggling to keep your head above water when the currents are against you.

Why? *Was it because the books were poorly translated?* No. I'm actually getting more positive reviews on Amazon.com than on the *.it*, (and I still don't understand why).

Some problem with keywords? No. Dagger 1, English version, is downloaded a lot more than its Italian brother, but book 2 still sells better in my homeland: on Amazon.it, for every 10-15 downloaded copies of Dagger 1, I sell one copy of Dagger 2. On the *.uk* is one every 25-30. On the *.com* is one every 40.

Why? Why? I wondered over and over again.

Then I saw something that had been under my eyes since always: my rankings. Independently from the downloaded copies, on the *.it* I'm a top 100 (a top gun!). On the *.uk* I'm a top 300, while on the *.com* I'm a top 3000 or something.

Do you think it matters? Of course it does.

In Italy I was (well, I still am) an authority of the sector. I was someone who got to the top, not somewhere around it. For instance, my small, independent, fantasy book was more downloaded than the free fantasy books of the biggest publishing house in my country, owned by Berlusconi himself, our former prime minister, (will that easily happen in USA, or England?). There were Italian blogs talking about me everywhere; googling around I found unknown readers suggesting Dagger in forums and facebook groups. The fact is that when people download Dagger in

Italy they will even *read* it. No joking. **Customers on Amazon.com may be so accustomed to free copies thrown in their faces that they download more books in a day that they will ever read in a lifetime.** But if I download a book that's on the top 100 general (and is on the fantasy podium) and has good reviews, I will probably read it, while I would probably download a book that's nr 2500 in the charts just because it's free and then I'll never read it, leaving it under the digital dust of my device (I've got thousands of them in my kindle, like all of you, probably).

So ask me again that question: Why work to sell internationally?Because in smaller markets you can become an *authority* in no time (or, at least, with less efforts). People will look for you, inform themselves about you and even *read* you if they see you there at the top. If you become an authority on the .com you may begin to sell your house and move to Hawaii, of course. But you've got everything to gain even in the smaller markets, believe me.

- **How to Get Your Book Translated the Right Way**

There are many ways to get your book translated. As for everything else in life, the cheapest ways are not often the best, but if we had all the money in this world to invest, then probably we'd *really* be in Hawaii, not here struggling to get our books translated. The key is in the middle.

First things first: Which (non-English) language will you choose? I'll get very specific here. I do think Amazon is here to last, and I mean everywhere in the world. The choices the Seattle company has made were made to change the books market forever and have a monopoly on it worldwide. So stick to them everywhere you can.

Amazon.it is a fast growing market, and the place where virtually the total amount of ebooks is sold in Italy. Paperbacks still sell better than ebooks, but things will change fast: if you conquer a good position on Amazon.it now, you'll probably keep it for a lifetime (more or less, it's what I'm trying to do. The concept of *long seller* will soon replace the one of *best seller*. Big publishing houses may sell 1000 copies of their book in a week and then nothing more. I prefer to sell ten copies everyday, but for a lifetime). This is why I consider to translate a book in Italian a good investment, as for French, even if it may take time to pay out.

The thing I would do (and actually will do soon) is to translate my books in Spanish. You have two growing, specific markets to conquer: *.es* and *.mx*, but also our loved *.com* (remember there are 45 millions of people who speak Spanish in the United States alone, and just think about Southern America... huge chances!).

I'd invest some money in that. Googling *spanish translation* may be a good beginning to pick up a name or two, but what I always do, even for what concerns editing, is to ask for a free sample – you send to your editor\translator a couple of pages and see what they do (if they accept, of course. Most will.) This will give you both a chance to know each other's work. You must always taste the quality of the final product, just don't put your book in the end of the first come.

The thing is, there's actually a good option to have your book translated in the language that you wish, (including afrikaans, if you fancy it) with *no initial cost*. It's http://www.babelcube.com/.

Give it a try. All the rules are there on the site, but mainly you have to give up a percentage of your royalties to the translator.

Personally, I would use it only with minor languages, but this is a personal opinion. I like to hire people to help me, pay them real money, be happy with the transaction and then have no more duty toward them, as they don't have toward me.

Of course this has a cost. But it's a *certain* cost.

- **Tips to Optimize for International Sales**

If you're still undecided whether (or how) to translate your book, mind that some great markets can be conquered even with your English language books: *.au*, for instance, or *.in*. They may not be great markets, but again: you have to think about what they will be ten years from now (especially India). Never stick to the present if you mean business. If you want to open a record store, go forward, I won't stop you.

I'm actually beginning to sell some on the German market, too, simply by (and that's my free tip for you) using another English version of Dagger with *German* keywords. Instead of *fantasy book*, write *fantasy bücher*. Instead of *war*, write *krieg* (you got the idea, right?). This will give you a lot of good chances there, take my word for granted. Germans are fluent in English, just like all northern European people, and I must say they are the kindest readers I ever had, too.

Focus on one market at a time. Join facebook groups localized in the country you wish to monetize and then move to somewhere else (use one copy with *french* keywords, you say? Well, it's definitely worth trying).

But I saved my super mega best tip for the end.

For our English markets, we all focus our keywords choosing on the *.com* (Kindle Samurai does that too, and all the kdp keywords processors out there). But remember? Amazon.com is a big, big pond, and it's easy to get lost in there. I actually obtained *very good* results choosing my keywords starting from the search bar of Amazon.co.uk, that is a middle way market (a middle way pond.) You know the process, I guess: type one word in the search bar and watch the result showing at the top of the list. *That* is the most searched keyword, and it surely differs from the equivalent on the *.com* market. Why do that? UK is a more manageable market, and it's not *that little*, too. Of course this may penalize your American market, or may not. Focus on the total amount of copies you sell, or download for free, and then decide.

Try, experiment, that's the only way to find out new things. Never stop being curious about this stuff.

- **Conclusion**

Never stick to mere numbers. Math and statistics have their rules, but too many people forget that we're talking about books, about feelings and drama, and those follow totally different rules; if they follow any, after all.

Ebook markets are growing everywhere and will continue to grow probably until the end of our life. Paper is dying. We may like it or not, but it's like this. I love vinyls. I love cds. But when I go out bicycling I use my Mp3 reader like everybody. So what I say is: become an authority *somewhere*, and do it *now*. Reserve your seat in the little markets, because with years they will grow, like the tree you planted in your garden as a child (well, I had a garden).

Yes. I definitely prefer to be a big fish in my little pond. Even because, with time, you can move to bigger ponds until you reach the ocean.

I'm Walt Popester, dark fantasy author and kdp coach. This is the book I've been talking about all the while: http://tinyurl.com/Dagger1freedownload.

Share knowledge, talk to people. Enjoy what you do and nobody will ever be like you.

Yours truly.

WP.

www.ingramcontent.com/pod-product-compliance
Lightning Source LLC
Chambersburg PA
CBHW051324220526

45468CB00004B/1487